One Another Christianity

by Roger Hillis

© 2018 One Stone Press.
All rights reserved. No part of this book may be reproduced in any form without written permission of the publisher.

Published by:
One Stone Press
979 Lovers Lane
Bowling Green, KY 42103

Printed in the United States of America

ISBN 13: 978-1-941422-30-4

www.onestone.com

Table of Contents

1. Members of One Another 5
2. Serving One Another 9
3. Care for One Another 13
4. Encouraging One Another 17
5. Greet One Another 21
6. Honor One Another 25
7. Forgive One Another 29
8. Be Hospitable to One Another 31
9. Do Not Speak Against One Another 35
10. Receive One Another 39
11. Be at Peace with One Another 43
12. Love One Another 47

The "One Another" Verses 51

Scripture quotations are taken from the New King James Version, copyright Thomas Nelson Publishers, 1979, 1980, 1982. Used by permission.

Lesson 1

Members of One Another

We are beginning a series of studies on the "one another" passages that describe our responsibilities and duties toward our fellow saints. The phrase "one another" is taken from the Greek word *allelon* which is found 58 times in the New Testament.

Let me make three important observations before we start.

1. **EVERY Christian must obey these "one another" commands.** These are not exclusively for the elders and others who are spiritually strong. These passages speak to all Christians about our responsibilities toward others. "Let nothing be done through selfish ambition or conceit; but in lowliness of mind let each esteem others better than himself. Let each of you look out not only for his own interests, but also for the interests of others" (Philippians 2:3-4). See also 2 Thessalonians 1:3 and Hebrews 6:10-11.

2. **Every Christian must fulfill ALL of these responsibilities.** As in all other areas of the Christian life, we cannot pick and choose which commands we like and which ones we will disregard. We cannot disobey any of God's commandments and still please Him. "For to this end I also wrote, that I might put you to the test, whether you are obedient in all things" (2 Corinthians 2:9). "Remind them to be subject to rulers and authorities, to obey, to be ready for every good work" (Titus 3:1).

3. **We must obey them in respect to EVERY OTHER Christian.** At least, to the best of our

Read the following passages and explain the figure of speech used to describe the Christian's relationship with God, Christ and/or other disciples.

Matthew 20:1–16
_____
_____

John 15:5
_____
_____

1 Corinthians 3:9
_____
_____

Galatians 6:10
_____
_____

Ephesians 2:19
_____
_____

Philippians 2:25
_____
_____

1 Peter 2:5
_____
_____

1 Peter 2:9
_____
_____

Today's study will focus on the statement that we are "members of one another." Read Romans 12:4-5 and Ephesians 4:25. What does that mean to you?

_____
_____
_____
_____
_____
_____
_____

Read 1 Corinthians 12:12-27. List some of the practical lessons we should learn from that passage for our lives together today in the church.

_____
_____
_____
_____
_____
_____
_____

ability and in keeping with our opportunities. We cannot select our best friends or our families or those who are more likeable than others. We must include everyone. Read James 2:1-9.

A local church is supposed to work together like an athletic team. Paul wrote in Philippians 1:27, "Only let your conduct be worthy of the gospel of Christ, so that whether I come and see you or am absent, I may hear of your affairs, that you stand fast in one spirit, with one mind striving together for the faith of the gospel."

The phrase "striving together" is an athletic term that refers to a spirit of cooperation, love, mutual respect and devotion. It points out that the relationship between two Christians is to be a friendship or, as the Bible describes it, a fellowship—sharing together of good times and bad.

Someone has said that coming together is a beginning, keeping together is progress, but working together is success. And that is the spirit of teamwork that we need to have in the local church. Another writer came up with the acrostic for TEAM: **T**ogether **E**veryone **A**chieves **M**ore.

"Now I plead with you, brethren, by the name of our Lord Jesus Christ, that you all speak the same thing, and that there be no divisions among you, but that you be perfectly joined together in the same mind and in the same judgment" (1 Corinthians 1:10).

That's what the Bible calls UNITY!

Explain these passages as they relate to the various members of the body and their differing functions.

- Romans 12:3-8 _____
_____
_____

- Ephesians 4:11 _____
  _____

- 1 Peter 4:10-11 _____
  _____

Thought Questions

1. Is there a difference in being a "member" somewhere and being "members of one another?" _____

2. Read Ephesians 4:1-3. Explain these words and phrases:
   - walk worthy _____
     _____

   - lowliness _____
     _____

   - gentleness _____
     _____

   - bearing with one another in love _____
     _____

   - endeavoring to keep the unity of the Spirit in the bond of peace
     _____

3. As with most Bible subjects, simply talking about being members of one another is not enough. How can we apply this principle to our lives together? _____
   _____

In this series, we are going to study about making everyone feel a part of the group, making every member an active, working, growing member, having no divisions in the body, caring for one another and bearing each other's burdens, having fun together, enjoying each other's company, being best friends, meeting everyone's needs—spiritual, moral, financial, and emotional, and breaking down any barriers that might exist.

Are YOU fulfilling your part of this "one another" responsibility?

8   One Another Christianity

Lesson 2

Serving One Another

Read Galatians 5:13

Definition: **SERVE**

Matthew 20:20-28

The contrast in this passage is between the way the world thinks and how we are to act in the Lord's kingdom.

In the kingdom of the world, people achieve greatness by dominating others. Best-selling books are titled *Looking Out for Number One* and *Winning Through Intimidation*. Without thinking of others, the world's elite step on as many as necessary to make it to the top.

That can even happen in religious circles. The scribes and Pharisees of Jesus' day had a problem with that (Matthew 23:5-12), as did Diotrephes (3 John 9-11).

But Jesus wants something different from us. He turns these carnal concepts upside down (as He does most things). True greatness comes through serving others. Even elders in the Lord's church are not to dominate and rule by force and decree, but by example (1 Peter 5:2-3).

1. What occasioned this discussion between Christ and the apostles? _____
_____

2. What does it mean to "lord it over" others?
_____
_____

Here are three key characteristics of a servant. (Discuss these in class.)

- **Put others' needs first.** The question should not be "What's in it for me?" but "what do THEY need?" See Philippians 2:1-4. People today focus on self; Jesus says think about the other person.

- **Prepare to be inconvenienced.** Opportunities to serve are often overlooked and undone because they are usually not convenient. Helping others takes time and effort (Luke 10:30-35). Anything that is truly worthwhile usually does!

- **Serve in unnoticed ways.** We must be involved in the day-to-day lives of others—helping, encouraging, praying, working, serving even if no one else knows about it (Matthew 6:1-4).

3. How did the Son of Man "serve" His fellow man?
   _____
   _____

4. What other lessons should we learn from these verses? _____
   _____
   _____

Thought Questions

John 13:1-17

1. Why did Jesus wash His disciples' feet? _____
   _____
   _____

2. Do verses 14-15 teach that we should wash each other's feet in the church today? _____

Ephesians 5:21

1. Is this verse talking only about wives? Explain your answer. _____
   _____
   _____

2. What does submission to one another have to do with serving others?_____
   _____
   _____

Philippians 2:1-4

1. What is the chief characteristic of one who puts others first?_____
   _____

> Each one should use whatever gift he has received to **serve others**, faithfully administering God's grace in its various forms.
>
> - 1 Peter 4:10, NIV

LESSON 2 Serving One Another 11

2. Why do so few people obey verse 4? _____
_____

Many children of God do not understand what is really involved in being a servant. Perhaps a few examples will serve to illustrate.

Serving is...

- Buying some groceries for a needy family.
- Inviting some less fortunate people to your home for a meal.
- Cooking some food and taking it to a family who needs it.
- Buying some clothing or a pair of shoes for someone who cannot afford them.
- Paying for some medicine for a sick child or an adult.
- Giving someone who cannot drive or who doesn't have car a ride to services.
- Sharing some vegetables from your garden with those who cannot grow their own.
- Buying a meal at a restaurant for someone who cannot afford to do so for you in return.
- Sharing some extra canned goods you will never eat with a family that needs it much more.
- Giving food to the hungry, drink to the thirsty, shelter to a stranger, clothing to the naked, medicine to the sick and visiting those in prison (Matthew 25:31-46).

List other examples of serving others: _____
_____
_____
_____
_____

Are YOU fulfilling your part of this "one another" responsibility?

Care for One Another

Lesson 3

Read 1 Corinthians 12:20-25

Definition: **CARE**

1 Corinthians 12:25

The apostle Paul tells the church at Corinth (and, by implication, us) that Christians are to care for one another. As we have noticed before, the church is to be a family and, as in all families, we are to love and provide for the needs of each other.

Another way to say that is to note that we are to be concerned about others, not merely ourselves. The same Greek word is used in Philippians 2:20. There Paul says that Timothy legitimately cared for other Christians (including those at Philippi), unlike so many others who cared only for self.

Paul tells us of his own concern for the churches he had established (2 Corinthians 11:28). Note that he felt that concern daily.

Interestingly, most of the time, the Bible tells us not to take care, be concerned about, or worry about things (see Matthew 6:25-34 and Philippians 4:6). In those places, we are told not to worry about material possessions, but rather, we are to trust God and He will provide!

But when it comes to our relationships in the kingdom of Christ, the Lord instructs us to **care** about and for each other.

Don't forget that this instruction was first given to the church at Corinth—a carnal, divided group of immature Christians (see 1 Corinthians 3:3). They were having all kinds of problems, and this letter

> But now indeed there are many members, yet one body. And the eye cannot say to the hand, "I have no need of you"; nor again the head to the feet, "I have no need of you." No, much rather, those members of the body which seem to be weaker are necessary. And those members of the body which we think to be less honorable, on these we bestow greater honor; and our unpresentable parts have greater modesty, but our presentable parts have no need. But God composed the body, having given greater honor to that part which lacks it, that there should be no schism in the body, but that the **members should have the same care for one another**.
>
> - 1 Corinthians 12:20-25

was sent to them by the apostle to try to straighten out some of those problems.

1 Corinthians 12:15 points out that there are to be no divisions in the body of Christ. At Corinth, some were proud and arrogant about the spiritual gifts they had been given by God. They thought themselves better than others. Others were jealous and bitter that their gifts were less significant (they thought) and that made them less important. He is showing them (and us) that there is no room for envy, strife, greed, pride, feelings of inferiority, and discord in the Lord's church.

Discuss these scriptures as they apply to this "one another" responsibility.

- Acts 4:32-37 _____
  _____

- Acts 6:1-6 _____
  _____

- Romans 12:15 _____
  _____

- James 1:26-27 _____
  _____

- Ecclesiastes 4:9-12 _____
  _____

A similar responsibility is found in the passage that teaches us to **bear one another's burdens** (Galatians 6:1-2). In the immediate context, he is talking about the burdens of sin. He follows up the teaching in chapter 5 about the battle between the works of the flesh and the fruit of the Spirit in the life of each individual, with a warning (6:1) that even Christians can be overtaken. Those who are spiritually minded are to help their brothers and sisters to be restored to the Lord when they have been weak and stumbled. This is surely one of the most difficult and unpleasant tasks that God has asked of us.

> Brethren, if a man is overtaken in any trespass, you who are spiritual restore such a one in a spirit of gentleness, considering yourself lest you also be tempted. **Bear one another's burdens**, and so fulfill the law of Christ.
>
> - Galatians 6:1-2

LESSON 3 Care for One Another

There is also a broader application of this principle. We are to help each other (because we care for one another) to carry or bear any burden of life that may be weighing on us.

Here are some examples:

- Those who are having marital difficulties
- Those who are struggling financially
- Parents whose children are rebelling
- Young people who are having a hard time
- Those who are not doing well in school
- Those who are lonely, depressed, upset, discouraged
- One who has just lost a job or is stuck in a job he/she hates
- One who has experienced a death in the family
- Those wrestling with drug or alcohol problems
- Those whose friends have let them down

List other examples: _____
_____
_____
_____
_____

Much of what we are talking about could be summarized by saying that we are to be best friends to each other. Read and comment on these passages about friends from the wisdom book called Proverbs.

- 1:10-11 _____
_____
_____

> A friend **loves at all times**, and a brother is born for adversity.
> - Proverbs 17:17
>
> A man who has friends must himself be friendly, but there is a friend who **sticks closer than a brother**.
> - Proverbs 18:24

- 12:26 _____
  _____

- 13:20 _____
  _____

- 17:17 _____
  _____

- 18:24 _____
  _____

- 22:24-25 _____
  _____

- 27:6 _____
  _____

- 27:17 _____
  _____

People are looking for a place to belong, a place where they fit in and are accepted as a friend and an equal. People want to be loved and to be a vital part of what is going on in life. They need a shelter from the storms of life and that is what the church is supposed to be!

Are YOU fulfilling your part of this "one another" responsibility?

Lesson 4

Encouraging One Another

"Therefore encourage one another, and build up one another, just as you also are doing" (1 Thessalonians 5:11, New American Standard Version).

Definition: **ENCOURAGE**

One of my favorite passages is Galatians 6:9: "And let us not grow weary while doing good, for in due season we shall reap if we do not lose heart." That is so helpful to me. I must admit that, at times, I grow discouraged and need a "shot in the arm" to keep me going. Sometimes, simply reading an uplifting passage like that one is all I need.

However, at times I need more. There are times when I need the encouragement that can come only from another disciple who lifts me up and gives me the strength I need. This lesson will discuss the responsibility we all have to "encourage one another."

Son of Encouragement

His name was Joseph (or Joses). But the apostles changed his name, giving him a "nickname" that fit his character and attitude of life. They called him Barnabas, which means "Son of Encouragement." What a name! Many people might be called "Grumpy" or "Sourpuss" or "Shorty." But how many people do you know who are so encouraging to others that they could be called son (or daughter) of encouragement?

Read these passages about Barnabas and list some of the ways in which he encouraged others.

- Acts 4:36-37 _____
  _____

The goal of encouragement is **"building up one another."**

We are supposed to be trying to help each other make it to heaven. What is the main tool we are to use in edifying and strengthening one another in the Lord's service? (Hint: see Acts 20:32.)

_____
_____

- Acts 9:26-27 _____
- Acts 11:19-24 _____
- Acts 15:36-37 _____

Discouraging One Another

Let's think for a moment about the opposite idea: discouraging one another. What would be some examples of things we might do that would tear others down spiritually, rather than building them up spiritually?

_____
_____
_____
_____
_____
_____

Several of the Proverbs show that we are to encourage one another with the words we speak to each other. Read these verses and make a brief comment on each:

- Proverbs 15:23 _____
- Proverbs 16:24 _____
- Proverbs 25:11 _____
- Proverbs 27:17 _____

Practical Applications

What are some specific ways we could encourage others?

- Send a card, thank you note or a small gift. And do so at totally unexpected times, not just on birthdays or anniversaries.
- Pick up the telephone and call someone, just to say "thanks" or to express your appreciation for something.
- Have a warm, positive atmosphere and attitude in all that you do. This reflects appreciation for people and for the blessings you have received from God.

LESSON 4 Encouraging One Another

- Be supportive and uplifting, especially when you know that others are hurting. That's when they need us most.

Your turn—list as many other specifics as you can.

- _____
- _____
- _____
- _____
- _____
- _____

Miscellaneous Verses

These verses contain the words "encourage," "consolation," "exhort," "edify," "comfort," etc. These are all the same idea. Read the verses and make a brief comment on each.

- Acts 15:31 _____
  _____

- Romans 1:12 _____
  _____

- Romans 14:19 _____
  _____

- 1 Thessalonians 2:10-12 _____
  _____

- Hebrews 3:12-13 _____
  _____

- Hebrews 6:18 _____
  _____

Are YOU fulfilling your part of this "one another" responsibility?

Greet One Another

("Salute one another," King James Version)

Read: Romans 16:16
1 Corinthians 16:20
2 Corinthians 13:12
1 Thessalonians 5:26
1 Peter 5:14

Definition: **GREET**

Read Romans 16:3-27.

Notice that Paul "greets" approximately 26 people by name, along with others who are unnamed (the church in their house; Rufus' mother, etc.). He also sends greetings from several others to people in Corinth (verses 21-23). Greeting was a common form of expressing love and appreciation for others and their contributions to the cause of Christ.

The Holy Kiss?

This is the part of this command that always gives us trouble. We dismiss it rapidly as being cultural and having no significance to today and that's that. But let's think about it for a moment.

Kissing was (and still is, in many cultures) a common form of greeting another or telling others goodbye. We still do the same in groups in which we feel especially close. Families, especially, will greet one another and tell one another farewell with a kiss. It is a natural thing to do, there is nothing sexual or perverse about it, and everyone feels comfortable doing it. Close friends often feel it is appropriate to express love and affection for others in this way. Even heads of state from Oriental countries will

Notice these other verses which emphasize greetings:
Philippians 4:21-22; Colossians 4:15; Titus 3:15; Hebrews 13:24; 3 John 13-14.

Important question: How seriously do we take the greeting of others?

The Specific or the Principle?

Is Paul binding the specific greeting of a holy kiss? Or is he simply telling them that when they greeted one another (in the way that was most commonly practiced then), it was to be holy and from a heart of love? I believe it to be the latter.

It seems to me, in many ways, to be parallel to the teaching in John 13:1-17 (which we studied already in lesson 2). He was not binding the practice of foot washing on the church for all time. He was using a common illustration of humility and service for others and tells us that we need to be humble and serve our fellow Christians.

In the same way, he is not requiring us to greet one another in an artificial or unnatural way. He is telling us to show that we care for and love one another in our sincere, heartfelt greeting of others.

treat one another in that way and may even do the same to visiting heads of state.

Would it be wrong for us to practice a greeting in this way today—with a sincere kiss on the cheek (with nothing sexual intended) or a hug of appreciation?

There are three examples of kisses in the New Testament. Read these accounts and describe which kisses were holy and which ones were not.

- Judas and Christ (Matthew 26:48-49) _____
  _____

- Father and Prodigal Son (Luke 15:20) _____
  _____

- Paul and the Ephesian elders (Acts 20:37) _____
  _____

Greet One Another with a HOLY Kiss

1. What is he saying by using the word "holy?"
   _____
   _____

2. What would be the opposite of holy? _____
   _____

3. Would the following greetings be holy or empty?

   "Hi. How are you?" (Oh, no, she's going to tell me.)
   _____
   _____

   "We are so glad to have you." (to a visitor while you are already thinking about getting out of the building so you can eat lunch) _____
   _____

"Thanks for calling; it's good to hear from you." (I hope you don't call again for another 12 years.) _____

_____

"It's so good to see you." (Whew! Get me out of here.) _____

_____

Thought Questions

1. What conclusions do you draw about the way we are to greet others?
   _____
   _____

2. What would be some of the ways we could disobey this command?
   _____
   _____

In the first century, greeting was a common form of expressing love and appreciation for others and their contributions to the cause of Christ. To greet someone was to acknowledge their worth, to welcome them, to let them know how much you loved them. It was more than a passing and meaningless, "Hi, how are you?" The old King James Version says, in most of those places, that we are to salute one another. The word salute carries with it the idea of respect for others that is included in the greeting.

It would be helpful to seek out those who are sitting alone or those who are not talking with anyone and then go up and start visiting with them. Let them know that you are really glad they are there. Make them feel important. Show them that you care.

As many times as it is mentioned in the Bible, this obviously is important to the Lord. We need to make certain that it is important to us also and that we greet one another in a way that will glorify our Father in heaven.

Are YOU fulfilling your part of this "one another" responsibility?

Lesson 6

Honor One Another

Read Romans 13:7

Definition: **HONOR**

God's Honor Roll

There are numerous people that the Bible tells us we are to honor. Read the scriptures listed below, tell **who** we are to honor and then tell **how** we should show honor to them.

Scripture	Who	How
John 5:22-23		
Romans 12:10		
1 Corinthians 12:22-24		
1 Corinthians 12:26		
Ephesians 6:2		
1 Timothy 1:17		
1 Timothy 5:3		
1 Timothy 5:17-18		
1 Timothy 6:1		
2 Timothy 2:20-21		
1 Peter 2:17		
1 Peter 3:7		

Render therefore to all their due: taxes to whom taxes are due, customs to whom customs, fear to whom fear, **honor to whom honor**.

- Romans 13:7

Be kindly affectionate to one another with brotherly love, in **honor** giving preference to one another.

- Romans 12:10

Seeking Honor

It is wrong to seek honor from others. Read the following verses and write down your thoughts from each about seeking honor and glory from others.

- Matthew 23:1-12 _____
  _____
  _____

- Mark 9:33-37 _____
  _____
  _____

- John 5:44 _____
  _____
  _____

Thought Questions

1. How long has it been since you honored another Christian in some way? _____
   _____

2. Re-read Romans 12:10. Explain the phrase "giving preference to one another." _____
   _____
   _____

Passages About Pride

Pride is one of the primary reasons why some do not honor others. Envy would be another. Some people feel worthy of any honor that is bestowed on someone else and therefore do not praise or honor others. Read and comment on these passages.

- Proverbs 13:10 _____
  _____

> But he who is greatest among you shall be your servant. And **whoever exalts himself will be humbled**, and he who humbles himself will be exalted.
>
> - Matthew 23:1-12

LESSON 6 Honor One Another

- Proverbs 27:2 _____
  _____

- Proverbs 29:23_____
  _____

- Galatians 5:26_____
  _____

- James 4:6_____
  _____

- 1 Peter 5:5-6 _____
  _____

- Philippians 2:3-4 _____
  _____

Are YOU fulfilling your part of this "one another" responsibility?

Lesson 7

Forgive One Another

Read Ephesians 4:32 and Colossians 3:13

As Christians, we are to be possessed by a spirit or attitude of forgiveness. Mistakes and misunderstandings with each other are inevitable. People *are* going to say and do some things wrong that will hurt and offend us. We must be prepared to forgive others so that we might be forgiven by them when we do wrong ourselves.

Examples of This Attitude

Read the passage listed, tell **who** forgave others and the circumstance.

- Acts 7:54-60 _____
  _____

- Romans 9:1-3 _____
  _____

- Luke 23:34 _____
  _____

Roadblocks to Forgiveness

Why would someone **not** forgive another? There could be several reasons (or excuses). Read the following passages and list some of those reasons.

- Ephesians 4:31-32 _____
  _____

- Galatians 6:1 _____
  _____

Our own forgiveness is conditioned on our willingness to forgive others.
Read Matthew 6:14-15 and Mark 11:25-26.

Read the following statements and tell (yes or no) if you think it describes true forgiveness.

"I'll forgive you but things will never be the same between us again." _____

"I'll forgive you but you will have to prove yourself to me." _____

"I'll forgive you but I'm going to keep my eye on you."
_____

"I'll forgive you but it will take a while for me to trust you again."
_____

- Matthew 18:21-22 _____
  _____

Think of other reasons why somebody would be unforgiving._____
_____

Think of some of the people God has forgiven:
- Zacchaeus (Luke 19:1-10)
- Woman caught in adultery (John 8:1-12)
- Thief on the cross (Luke 23:39-43)
- Peter, after denying Jesus and swearing (Mark 14:66-72)
- Saul of Tarsus (Acts 8:3; 9:1-2)

List other examples from the Bible: _____
_____
_____

God is a Forgiver

All of this reminds us that we serve a forgiving God. Read the following passages.

Psalm 32:1-2

Psalm 51:1-4

Psalm 103:8-13

Psalm 145:8-9

Isaiah 1:18

Isaiah 38:17

Isaiah 55:6-7

Micah 7:18-19

1 John 1:8-9

Thought Questions

1. Read the parable in Matthew 18:23-35. What lessons can we learn from this passage?
   _____
   _____

2. In Ephesians 4:26, what time limit does the Lord place on resolving problems with others?
   _____

3. Read and comment on Luke 17:3._____
   _____
   _____

"Forgiveness and bitterness are the choices. Forgiveness feels better."

Are YOU fulfilling your part of this "one another" responsibility?

Lesson 8

Be Hospitable to One Another

Read 1 Peter 4:9, Hebrews 13:1-2, and Romans 12:13

Definition: **HOSPITALITY**

Bible Examples

Read the accounts listed below and tell who practiced the hospitality, to whom and the circumstances.

- Genesis 18:1-8 _____
  _____

- 1 Kings 17:8-16 _____
  _____

- 2 Kings 4:8-11 _____
  _____

- Acts 4:32-35 _____
  _____

- Acts 16:14-15 _____
  _____

- 2 Timothy 1:16-18 _____
  _____

Thought Questions

1. In Romans 12:13, what does "given to" hospitality mean? _____
   _____

> Be **hospitable** to one another without grumbling.
> - 1 Peter 4:9
>
> Let **brotherly love** continue. Do not forget to **entertain strangers**, for by so doing some have unwittingly entertained angels.
> - Hebrews 13:1-2
>
> ...distributing to the needs of the saints, given to **hospitality**.
> - Romans 12:13

2. Why is hospitality a qualification of an elder (1 Timothy 3:2)? _____
_____

3. In Hebrews 13:1-2, does that mean we might actually see and eat with angels today?_____
_____

4. In 1 Peter 4:9, explain the phrase, "without grumbling." _____
_____
_____

Hospitality is...

- having a party so the young people will have some wholesome entertainment.
- inviting visitors to your home for a snack after services.
- keeping the preacher during a gospel meeting.
- having a wiener roast in your back yard.
- sharing a sandwich or a bowl of soup with a friend who stops in at mealtime.
- opening your home to friends who are just passing through town.
- rearranging the furniture in your living room for a gospel sing.
- having out-of-town Christians who visit services on Sunday morning into your home for the noon meal—unexpectedly.
- inviting Christians and non-Christians over to your house for a Bible study.
- being friendly to all who come your way.
- doing "good to all, especially to those who are of the household of faith" (Galatians 6:10).

Your Turn

List other ways of showing hospitality.

_____
_____
_____
_____
_____
_____
_____
_____

LESSON 8 Be Hospitable to One Another

No Hospitality for These

There are some people to whom the Lord says we should **not** show hospitality.

- 1 Corinthians 5:11 _____

- 2 Thessalonians 3:10 _____

- 2 John 9-11 _____

Are YOU fulfilling your part of this "one another" responsibility?

Lesson 9

Do Not Speak Against One Another

Read James 4:11 and 5:9

It is vitally important that we speak properly to each other. Words have tremendous power to build up or to destroy. As we seek to help one another grow into the image of Christ, we must use caution not to destroy the Lord's work with our mouths. Too often, we speak without thinking about the consequences. There are many verses that deal with this subject and we must heed these warnings.

Define These Words

Murmuring _____
_____
_____

Lying _____
_____
_____

Slander _____
_____
_____

Gossip _____
_____
_____

Backbiting _____
_____
_____

> **Do not speak evil of one another, brethren.** He who speaks evil of a brother and judges his brother, speaks evil of the law and judges the law. But if you judge the law, you are not a doer of the law but a judge.
>
> - James 4:11

A Special Warning

As Christians, we ought not to make or listen to unprovable accusations against others. That is inappropriate behavior for a Christian. But it is especially important not to do so against a church leader. See 1 Timothy 5:19. (If there are witnesses to the sin, proceed with caution—1 Timothy 5:20-21.)

Why do you think this warning is given?

_____
_____
_____
_____

What should you do if someone persists in spreading false rumors about the elders?

_____
_____
_____
_____

Whisperings _____
_____
_____

Verses About Speaking

Read these verses and comment on them as they apply to the subject of our lesson.

- Matthew 12:34-37 _____
_____
_____

- Romans 16:18 _____
_____
_____

- 2 Corinthians 12:20 _____
_____
_____

- Ephesians 4:29 _____
_____
_____

- Philippians 2:14 _____
_____
_____

- 2 Timothy 2:16 _____
_____
_____

- James 3:3-12 _____
_____
_____

- 1 Peter 4:15 _____
_____
_____

Thought Questions

1. Read Ephesians 5:4. List the three types of speech condemned there and define each.
   _____
   _____
   _____
   _____

2. Explain the phrase "not double-tongued" in 1 Timothy 3:8. _____
   _____

3. How can we put a stop to ungodly speech against our brothers and sisters? _____
   _____
   _____

4. Read Galatians 5:19-21. Which of the "works of the flesh" could involve speech? _____
   _____
   _____

While we are talking about our speech, let's discuss the subject of speaking to one another.

There are a number of types of speech that the Bible warns us against, as far as how we speak to our fellow Christians. Read these verses, then list and define these improper kinds of speech.

- 1 Peter 3:9 _____
  _____
  _____

- Ephesians 4:25_____
  _____
  _____

One Additional Thought…

It is bad enough that we sometimes speak against one another **to** one another. But it is very foolish and damaging to the cause of Christ when we speak **about** other Christians to outsiders! Some of the problems we have in trying to convert people lies in the fact that their opinion of the church is not too great and sometimes that has happened because of things that Christians have said about their fellow disciples. We must exercise extreme caution not to verbally run down the church in front of non-Christians.

- Ephesians 4:26 _____
  _____
  _____

- Ephesians 4:31 _____
  _____
  _____

Are YOU fulfilling your part of this "one another" responsibility?

Lesson 10

Receive One Another

Read Romans 15:5-7

When it comes to relationships in the church, everyone is to be included, everyone. There are not supposed to be any insiders and outsiders, any have and have-nots in the church. We are all one in Christ Jesus. That's one of the unique qualities of Christianity that distinguishes it from other world religions. Everyone is equal in the eyes of the Lord.

Church growth material refers to the process of welcoming new members as "assimilation." One of the primary differences between growing churches and those that are shrinking is how they deal with new members. Most churches can bring people in the front door. Growing churches have learned some secrets about how to close the back door. There are three keys to understanding how to assimilate new people into the fellowship of a local church. This lesson will take a brief look at these three keys.

Thought Questions

1. Read Galatians 3:26-29 and list some of the distinctions that do not exist in the body of Christ. _____
   _____
   _____

2. To whom were the apostles to preach in order to fulfill the Great Commission (Mark 16:15-16)?
   _____
   _____

> Now may the God of patience and comfort grant you to be like-minded toward one another, according to Christ Jesus, that you may with one mind and one mouth glorify the God and Father of our Lord Jesus Christ. Therefore **receive one another**, just as Christ also received us, to the glory of God.
>
> - Romans 15:5-7

3. In Acts 6, what was the problem and how was it solved? _____
   _____
   _____

4. Returning to our text in Romans 15, the apostle tells the early disciples to receive one another, in spite of their differences. What two major challenges do chapters 14 and 15 deal with? _____
   _____
   _____
   _____

Receive One Another

We are to accept others as our spiritual equals, even if they are different from us in some way. When Jesus died on the cross, He did so for everybody. He did not die for a select few, although there will be many who reject God's gracious offer of salvation (see Hebrews 2:9; Titus 2:11-14).

One of the first principles of God's dealing with mankind is that He shows no partiality or favoritism (Acts 10:34-35). If we are going to be His children, then we must act the same. If we show partiality or respect of persons, we are guilty before God of grievous sin (James 2:1-9).

Consider One Another

Read Hebrews 10:23-25. Define the five verbs (action words) that deal with the mutual responsibilities that Christians have toward one another and make some comments on how they apply to this study.

Hold fast_____
_____

Consider one another _____
_____

Stir up love and good works_____
_____

Do not forsake the assembling_____
_____

Exhort one another _____
_____

Be Devoted to One Another

Read Romans 12:10 (especially in the New American Standard Version, if you have one).

What does it mean to be devoted to someone else? _____
_____

What did Peter mean when he referred to our "like precious faith" (2 Peter 1:1)?
_____

If We Knew Each Other Better

If we knew each other better,
We would praise where we now blame,
We would know each bears his burden,
Wears some hidden cross of shame.
We would feel the heartaches bitter
They so long alone have borne.
If we knew each other better,
We would praise instead of scorn.
If we knew each other better,
You and I and all the rest,
Seeing down beneath the surface
To the sorrows all unguessed,
We would quit our cold complaining,
And a hand of trust extend,
If we knew each other better,
We would count each one a friend.
We can know each other better
If we take the time to try,
Little deeds of loving kindness,
Make a better by and by.
Just a look of understanding
Brings a touch of all mankind;
We can know each other better
Yes, seeking, we shall find.

(Author unknown)

Are YOU fulfilling your part of this "one another" responsibility?

Lesson 11

Be at Peace with One Another

Read 1 Thessalonians 5:12-13, Mark 9:50

Our next study of the "one another" responsibilities is the command to "be at peace" with each other. In the most famous of all sermons, the Sermon on the Mount, Jesus said, "Blessed are the peacemakers, For they shall be called sons of God" (Matthew 5:9). Notice that the Lord did not promise happiness to peace *lovers*, peace *talkers*, or peace *dreamers*, but to peace *makers*.

Things Which Make for Peace

"Therefore let us pursue the things which make for peace and the things by which one may edify another" (Romans 14:19). We must actively look for and pursue peace in the local church.

Read Ephesians 4:1-3. Define the following words or phrases.

Lowliness _____
_____
_____

Gentleness _____
_____
_____

Longsuffering _____
_____
_____

Bearing with one another _____
_____
_____

The Lord Desires Peace

Five times in the New Testament, God is called "the God of peace" (Romans 15:33; 16:20; Philippians 4:9; 1 Thessalonians 5:23; Hebrews 13:20). Jesus was prophetically referred to as "the Prince of peace" (Isaiah 9:6). The word "peace" is found in every book of the New Testament, eighty eight times in all. God clearly wants His people to serve Him together in peace and harmony.

Benefits of Peace

There are two benefits to be derived from being a people at peace with God and one another.

First, it leads to a blessed life here. The beatitude says that those who are peacemakers will be called "the sons of God." Philippians 4:7 promises us that "the peace of God, which surpasses all understanding, will guard your hearts and minds through Christ Jesus."

Second, and most importantly, it leads to eternal life in heaven. "Pursue peace with all men, and holiness, without which no one will see the Lord." (Hebrews 12:14). Those who seek peace will be rewarded eternally by the Lord.

Read Ephesians 4:32 and define these terms.

Being kind _____

_____

Being tenderhearted _____

_____

Forgiveness _____

_____

Notice that these are qualities of the heart, inner attitudes that radiate from a disciple's love for God and his fellow man.

Thought Questions

What do these verses teach about peace?

- John 17:11, 20-23 _____
  _____

- 1 Corinthians 1:10 _____
  _____

- 1 Corinthians 3:3 _____
  _____

- 1 Thessalonians 5:12-13 _____
  _____

- Romans 12:18 _____
  _____

Things Which Destroy Peace

Read the following verses and list those things which the Bible says can destroy the peace and harmony that the Lord desires.

- Ephesians 4:31 _____
  _____
  _____

- Galatians 5:15 _____

- Galatians 5:26 _____

- 2 Timothy 2:23 _____

- James 1:19-20 _____

- 3 John 9-10 _____

We must always remember that the enemy is the devil—not each other. Our adversary would like nothing better than to get the people of God fighting among themselves, because when we do that, we won't be spending much time trying to save the lost.

Making Peace With God

There is a sense in which the responsibility to be peacemakers refers to our duty to teach the gospel to the lost, thereby making people at peace with the Lord.

Explain how each of these verses mentions peace and evangelism.

- Romans 10:15 _____

- Ephesians 2:17-18 _____

- Ephesians 6:15 _____

Are YOU fulfilling your part of this "one another" responsibility?

Lesson 12

Love One Another

Read John 15:12, 17 and Romans 13:8

Definition: **LOVE**

The most often repeated "one another" commandment from the Lord is the responsibility for Christians to "love one another." In some ways, this duty and privilege summarizes all of the other "one another" obligations. This lesson should help us learn how to obey and carry out this awesome responsibility.

Brotherly Love

Here are some of the ways we can show our love for each other.

Hospitality is a good way to share our love with others. And it is a command of God (Romans 12:13). Invite other Christians into your home.

Spending time together helps love to grow. Families should spend time with other families. When we spend too much time with non-Christians and not enough time with other Christians, we grow weak spiritually. The early Christians spent much time with one another.

Caring, not complaining, will show our love. Build up; do not tear down. Encourage; do not discourage. We should try to be a spiritual source of joy and comfort to each other.

Remember that brotherly love should be a two-way street. Do not just be a "user." Be a giver of love to others. Even when others don't act like they should, continue to love them. Don't forget that God loved us while we were still sinners (Romans 5:8).

Love

Although I talk about love, if I am not showing it by kindness, it means nothing. Even if I attend all the services, sing without an instrument and observe the Lord's Supper every Sunday, if I don't have love, I am in real spiritual trouble. And if I preach lots of sermons, teach Bible classes, grade Bible correspondence courses, am appointed as an elder or a deacon, but don't really love my brothers and sisters, I won't go to heaven.

- 1 Corinthians 13:1-3, paraphrased by Roger Hillis

"What does love look like? It has the hands to help others. It has the feet to hasten to the poor and needy. It has eyes to see misery and want. It has ears to hear the sighs and sorrows of men. That is what love looks like." (Augustine)

List some other practical ways in which we can show our love for one another.

_____
_____
_____

> There is a legend about John and his last days on earth. It is said that he was returned from his exile on Patmos to Ephesus where he served the church until his death. In his frailty, he would stand before the church to preach and say **"Little children, love one another."**
>
> And that was his entire sermon.

Thought Questions

1. In 1 Peter 4:8, define the word "fervent." _____
_____
_____

2. In Hebrews 10:24, how do you "stir up love" in another person? _____
_____
_____

Passages About Love

Read and comment on these verses:

- 1 Thessalonians 4:9-10 _____
_____

- Hebrews 13:1-3 _____
_____

- 1 Peter 1:22-23 _____
_____

- 1 Peter 3:8-9 _____
_____

- 2 Peter 1:5-7 _____
_____

LESSON 12 Love One Another   49

Consequences of a Lack of Love

Read these verses and discuss what they teach will result from a lack of love:

- 1 John 3:10 _____
  _____

- 1 John 3:14 _____
  _____

- 1 John 4:7-8 _____
  _____

- 1 John 4:11-12 _____
  _____

The Apostle of Love

The apostle John is often referred to as the apostle of love. He is believed to be the person called "the disciple whom Jesus loved" (John 13:23 and others). He says much about the need for love in his letters. Read these verses and comment on them:

- 1 John 3:11 _____
  _____

- 1 John 3:16-18 _____
  _____

- 1 John 3:23 _____
  _____

- 1 John 4:20-5:2 _____
  _____

- 2 John 5 _____
  _____

There are far too many passages about love for us to cover them all in one short lesson. If you have a favorite Bible verse about love, list it here and share your thoughts with the rest of the class. _____

Are YOU fulfilling your part of this "one another" responsibility?

The "One Another" Verses

Mark 9:50
"Salt is good, but if the salt loses its flavor, how will you season it? Have salt in yourselves, and have peace with one another."

John 13:14
"If I then, your Lord and Teacher, have washed your feet, you also ought to wash one another's feet."

John 13:34
"A new commandment I give to you, that you love one another; as I have loved you, that you also love one another."

John 13:35
"By this all will know that you are My disciples, if you have love for one another."

John 15:12
"This is My commandment, that you love one another as I have loved you."

John 15:17
"These things I command you, that you love one another."

Romans 12:5
"So we, being many, are one body in Christ, and individually members of one another."

Romans 12:10
"Be kindly affectionate to one another with brotherly love, in honor giving preference to one another."

Romans 12:16
"Be of the same mind toward one another. Do not set your mind on high things, but associate with the humble. Do not be wise in your own opinion."

Romans 13:8
"Owe no one anything except to love one another, for he who loves another has fulfilled the law."

Romans 14:13
"Therefore let us not judge one another anymore, but rather resolve this, not to put a stumbling block or a cause to fall in our brother's way."

Romans 15:5
"Now may the God of patience and comfort grant you to be like-minded toward one another, according to Christ Jesus."

Romans 15:7
"Therefore receive one another, just as Christ also received us, to the glory of God."

Romans 15:14
"Now I myself am confident concerning you, my brethren, that you also are full of goodness, filled with all knowledge, able to admonish one another."

Romans 16:16
"Greet one another with a holy kiss. The churches of Christ greet you."

1 Corinthians 11:33
"Therefore, my brethren, when you come together to eat, wait for one another."

1 Corinthians 12:25
"That there should be no schism in the body, but that the members should have the same care for one another."

1 Corinthians 16:20
"All the brethren greet you. Greet one another with a holy kiss."

2 Corinthians 13:12
"Greet one another with a holy kiss."

Galatians 5:13
"For you, brethren, have been called to liberty; only do not use liberty as an opportunity for the flesh, but through love serve one another."

Galatians 5:15
"But if you bite and devour one another, beware lest you be consumed by one another!"

Galatians 5:17
"For the flesh lusts against the Spirit, and the Spirit against the flesh; and these are contrary to one another, so that you do not do the things that you wish."

Galatians 5:26
"Let us not become conceited, provoking one another, envying one another."

Galatians 6:2
"Bear one another's burdens, and so fulfill the law of Christ."

Ephesians 4:2
"With all lowliness and gentleness, with longsuffering, bearing with one another in love."

Ephesians 4:25
"Therefore, putting away lying, each one speak truth with his neighbor, for we are members of one another."

Ephesians 4:32
"And be kind to one another, tenderhearted, forgiving one another, just as God in Christ also forgave you."

Ephesians 5:19
"Speaking to one another in psalms and hymns and spiritual songs, singing and making melody in your heart to the Lord."

Ephesians 5:21
"Submitting to one another in the fear of God."

Colossians 3:9
"Do not lie to one another, since you have put off the old man with his deeds."

Colossians 3:13
"Bearing with one another, and forgiving one another, if anyone has a complaint against another, even as Christ forgave you, so you also must do."

Colossians 3:16
"Let the word of Christ dwell in you richly in all wisdom, teaching and admonishing one another in psalms and hymns and spiritual songs, singing with grace in your hearts to the Lord."

1 Thessalonians 3:12
"And may the Lord make you increase and abound in love to one another and to all, just as we do to you."

1 Thessalonians 4:9
"But concerning brotherly love you have no need that I should write to you, for you yourselves are taught by God to love one another."

1 Thessalonians 4:18
"Therefore comfort one another with these words."

1 Thessalonians 5:11
"Therefore comfort each other and edify one another, just as you also are doing."

Titus 3:3
"For we ourselves were also once foolish, disobedient, deceived, serving various lusts and pleasures, living in malice and envy, hateful and hating one another."

Hebrews 3:13
"But exhort one another daily, while it is called "Today," lest any of you be hardened through the deceitfulness of sin."

Hebrews 10:24
"And let us consider one another in order to stir up love and good works."

Hebrews 10:25
"Not forsaking the assembling of ourselves together, as is the manner of some, but exhorting one another, and so much the more as you see the Day approaching."

James 4:11
"Do not speak evil of one another, brethren. He who speaks evil of a brother and judges his brother, speaks evil of the law and judges the law. But if you judge the law, you are not a doer of the law but a judge."

James 5:9
"Do not grumble against one another, brethren, lest you be condemned. Behold, the Judge is standing at the door!"

James 5:16
"Confess your trespasses to one another, and pray for one another, that you may be healed. The effective, fervent prayer of a righteous man avails much."

1 Peter 1:22
"Since you have purified your souls in obeying the truth through the Spirit in sincere love of the brethren, love one another fervently with a pure heart."

1 Peter 3:8
"Finally, all of you be of one mind, having compassion for one another; love as brothers, be tenderhearted, be courteous."

1 Peter 4:8
"And above all things have fervent love for one another, for 'love will cover a multitude of sins.'"

1 Peter 4:9
"Be hospitable to one another without grumbling."

1 Peter 4:10
"As each one has received a gift, minister it to one another, as good stewards of the manifold grace of God."

1 Peter 5:5
"Likewise you younger people, submit yourselves to your elders. Yes, all of you be submissive to one another, and be clothed with humility, for 'God resists the proud, but gives grace to the humble.'"

1 Peter 5:14
"Greet one another with a kiss of love. Peace to you all who are in Christ Jesus. Amen."

1 John 1:7
"But if we walk in the light as He is in the light, we have fellowship with one another, and the blood of Jesus Christ His Son cleanses us from all sin."

1 John 3:11
"For this is the message that you heard from the beginning, that we should love one another."

1 John 3:23
"And this is His commandment: that we should believe on the name of His Son Jesus Christ and love one another, as He gave us commandment."

1 John 4:7
"Beloved, let us love one another, for love is of God; and everyone who loves is born of God and knows God."

1 John 4:11
"Beloved, if God so loved us, we also ought to love one another."

1 John 4:12
"No one has seen God at any time. If we love one another, God abides in us, and His love has been perfected in us."

2 John 5
"And now I plead with you, lady, not as though I wrote a new commandment to you, but that which we have had from the beginning: that we love one another."

More than Anything Else

As flowers and grass must fade and die,
So, some day, must you and I.
Resurrection begins our life anew;
I want to go to heaven.
I hope you do, too.

Before too long, we all shall be
face to face with eternity,
When God will give us our just due.
I want to go to heaven.
I hope you do, too.

All mankind will assemble there;
Each person's fate will God declare;
The lost will be many, the saved ones, few.
I hope to go to heaven.
I hope you do, too.

When I stand to be judged upon that day,
I hope to hear my Savior say,
"Faithful servant, you've been true,
Enter into heaven."
I hope you will, too.

(Jean Blackford, Owensboro, KY)

www.ingramcontent.com/pod-product-compliance
Lightning Source LLC
Chambersburg PA
CBHW070452050426
42451CB00015B/3445